The new baby

Story by Beverley Randell
Illustrated · by Ernest Papps

Tom came home after school.

"Hello, Grandpa," he said.
"Where is Mom?
 Where is Grandma?"

"Mom is at the hospital,"
said Grandpa.
"The baby is coming.
Dad is with Mom.
Grandma is with Mom, too.
I am staying here with you."

"I am cooking fish,"
said Grandpa.

"I'll help you," said Tom.
"I like cooking."

Tom went to bed. He went to sleep.

Grandpa went to sleep, too.

Ring, ring,
went the phone.

Grandpa woke up. Tom woke up.

"Hello, hello," said Grandpa.

Grandpa shouted,
"A girl! The baby is a girl!
Baby Emma is here."

Tom shouted,
"A girl! A girl!"

Grandpa and Tom
went to the hospital
to see Mom and Emma.

"I'm going to help you.
I'll take care of Emma, too,"
said Tom.

"I like little babies," said Tom.

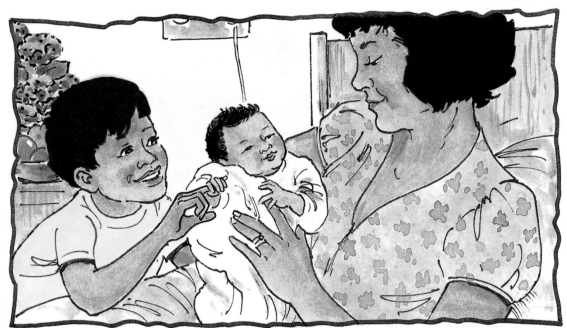